Christmas in Monmouthshire

Carol Ann Lewis

OTHER BOOKS BY CAROL ANN LEWIS

FICTION

HANBURY PARK
EDINA GREEN: IN THE AFTERLIFE

NON FICTION

CWMBRAN HISTORY AND MYSTERY
GWENT HISTORY AND MYSTERY
VICTORIAN CWMBRAN
VICTORIAN PONTYPOOL
VICTORIAN DOMESTIC ABUSE
HAUNTING TALES
TELL THEM OF US
CHILDREN OF NATURE A HISTORY OF WITCHES
DREAMS THE FORGOTTEN CRAFT

ALL AVAILABLE FROM AMAZON OR AS A DOWNLOAD TO
KINDLE

FIRST SIGNS

It's hard to imagine that at the beginning of the 19th century, Christmas was barely celebrated. It existed in name only and was not considered a holiday in the way it is today. It had been banned in the time of Cromwell and although all legislation against it had been dropped once the monarchy was restored, it never regained its pre Cromwell popularity. As a result many customs and Christmas characters were lost. You only have to look at the front pages of local newspaper the Monmouthshire Merlin to see how the holiday became almost non-existent and how it rose again to the celebration we know today.

Modern day preparations for Christmas begin when cards start creeping on to shop shelves around September. In the Monmouthshire Merlin of 5th December 1829, there was no mention of Christmas whatsoever. The following week there appeared one advertisement specifically aimed at Christmas and that was for pocket books and literary annuals for the new year. There also appeared a small article about the decline of Christmas.

"Shall we pass without comment the approach of Christmas?" it asked, "We have no longer a Christmas. It is now but a name, the recollection of a delightful dream, the memory of a joyous pageant whose gaiety and excitement are no more".

Also in the Merlin, in 1836 was a poem mourning the loss of Christmas.

"Sing a mournful song for Christmas
We have no Christmas now
Sing a mournful song for Christmas
Beneath the holly bough

The world has lost its childhood
Its hair is touched with grey
Oh sing beneath the holly
How mirth is passed away.

The rich and poor are strangers
They live too far apart
There is snow upon the housetops
And snow too in the heart

No pleasure is in common
And never ties can bind
Like joys they share together
Man's soul unto his kind.

Where is the ancient Yule log
That lit the ancient hearth?
Have tales and jest, like fairies
Forsaken our dull earth.

Hang up no more the mistletoe
As in the olden time
When blush and smile beneath it
Made sudden summer clime.

Too heavily the present
Is felt upon our day
Ours is the age of iron

With the gilding worn away.

Sing a mournful song for Christmas
We have no Christmas now
Sing a mournful song for Christmas
Beneath the holly bough.

The extent as to which Christmas was dying out can be seen in a notice placed in the Monmouthshire Merlin on December 15th 1838. It read -

"We the grocers of Abergavenny and Blaenavon most sincerely return thanks to the public for the liberal support with which we have been favoured and respectfully inform our friends that in consequence of small profits and the frequent impositions practised upon us at this season of the year we are obliged to discontinue the usual Christmas boxes".

A similar notice was printed in the Monmouth Gazette for 1847.

"Grocers have resolved to discontinue the annoying and troublesome practice of giving Christmas presents but intend to bestow an equal amount of money for the benefit of the poor in contribution to charities."

The newspaper continued to say it -

"hardly regretted the decline of the custom now that the goodwill with which it originated has gone, for as tradesmen sell for profit, the cost is added to their expenses"

The turnaround began in the 1840's, though Clement Clarke Moore had already written his poem 'A Visit from St Nicholas', also known as 'The Night Before Christmas' in 1823. Charles Dickens published 'A Christmas Carol', when for most, Christmas was just another workday. How was Scrooge, or anyone, expected to keep Christmas, when there was no Christmas to keep? The visits of the ghosts show him it wasn't too late to change, Christmas could be saved. Before this book was published though, on 2nd January 1836, the Monmouthshire Merlin ran an article on keeping Christmas.

"The only way to keep Christmas, is not to keep it to ourselves. To realise it, we must disperse it, to enjoy it we must confer it on others ... Merry is their Christmas who, with young and old about them can sit in the centre and enjoy the blaze of a fire almost too large for comfort. But merrier is theirs whose hospitality is not confined to their own hearths, not shut in by doors and windows, but extends, as in olden days, to those without, who in this joyous and generous season are gathered together in homes otherwise blank and barren of the commonest enjoyment. As in the olden time, and in ours also. To all who welcome the return of Christmas it must be one of the most cheering of its reflections that the rich and the noble of the land still observe this richest and noblest of Christmas customs by widening the ordinary boundaries of hospitality and inviting the humble dependents to a feast rendered a thousand times more sweet by a kindly sympathy"

The emphasis on celebrating Christmas was with food to begin with, Newport Market never boasted a more noble display according to the Monmouthshire Merlin of 1844. The meat was well fed and cleanly dressed. Mr Duckham displayed twenty two quarters of prime beef with eight inches of thick fat! There were also pigs, sheep and goats, fowls, duck, turkeys and geese. The confectioners shops sold currants and raisins covered in cinnamon and figs and lumps of sugar coated in ginger.

Then, in 1848, the London Illustrated News published a drawing of Queen Victoria, Prince Albert and family around their Christmas tree. The popularity of Christmas, both as a holiday and commercially, would begin to soar.

Christmas markets were advertised but they were a regular occurrence anyway and mainly concentrated on meat. The produce available at Pontypool Market was mentioned in December 1848.

"Our market was well supplied with delicacies of the season and it was generally acknowledged that better meat, geese were never exhibited in Pontypool. Mr William Jones seemed determined to keep up his reputation by the excellence of his show, he slaughtered a prize heifer, fed and bred by Capel Hanbury Leigh which attracted much attention. The only complaint heard was scarcity of cash amongst purchasers."

In 1851 the Monmouthshire Merlin published an advertisement promoting products for personal attraction – hair oil, skin cream and tooth cleaning powder- aimed at people attending Christmas parties. By 1853, Christmas was a holiday, businesses were informing the public of their days of closure such as this one.

"Christmas! The public are respectfully informed the tradesmen of Newport have agreed to keep their establishments closed on December 26th to give their assistants an opportunity to visit friends at Christmas".

Another advertisement drew attention to party wear – head dresses, caps and gloves – and James Ewin had reduced the price of his monster almond seed Christmas cake to one shilling and two pence per pound. This monster cake was described in the Merlin of 23 December 1853.

"No season of festivity appears to be allowed to pass without Mr James Ewins, Commercial Street, making a monster cake! This one on which stands a Christmas tree laden with bon bons has every leaf glittering with silver".

It was thirteen feet in circumference, had a depth of eighteen inches and weighed five hundred pounds. Its surface was covered in almond paste weighing sixty pounds and no 'deleterious colours' were used. The tree was designed by Mr Ewins but made by Smith and Co. of London. Six imperial lions led beneath the shadow of the tree.

1855 saw Christmas gifts start to be advertised for

example bibles with gilt rims, books such as 'Charades for the Drawing Room', and popular music at three pence a sheet.

Shopkeepers began to make an effort in making their window displays enticing. In 1857 the Merlin reported butchers busy getting stock ready for a Christmas show. Grocers were decorating their windows and introducing a sprig of holly to make their stock more attractive, while confectioners were decorating their stock with tinsel.

Villiers and Andrews were offering photographic portraits as presents from one shilling each in 1857 and pantomimes were advertised in 1858 at various theatres, mostly fairy tales – Robin Hood, Red Riding Hood etc · but one theatre was showing 'The Siege of Troy'.

Not everyone could afford what was being displayed in shop windows of course and the gap between rich and poor was noted in the Monmouthshire Merlin on 20th December 1862.

"Shops assuming a festive appearance. The good things in life are displayed in rich profusion; and the only regret one feels in walking the streets is that everybody cannot have a share of the provision our tradesmen have made."

It went on to describe the confectioners shops filled with 'luscious compounds', grocery shops with rich fruits made to look richer by artistically designed cases in which they were held and holly branches bending under the weight of berries.

By 1863 the tradesmen of Newport were closing their premises for a greater amount of time, from Thursday the 24th December until Monday the 28th in this year.

By now Christmas was starting to become more elaborate. In 1864, H J Groves advertised his pianofortes, a major purchase. Blands of Commercial Street, Newport, were selling mince pies and E Fennel's was putting on a fat turkey show as well as selling geese and duck.

Christmas novelties appeared in 1865. R P Napper, Newport, was selling gifts from London and Paris such as tree ornaments, magic flowers and preserved fruit. He was also supplying parties with a musical stand that played several tunes. Seasonal cards were on sale and new for 1867 were musical photo albums and children's books.

In 1866, J Ewins was advertising his large ornamental almond iced Christmas cake which you could buy at one shilling and four pence per pound. The following year he branched into cases of spirits. For sixteen shillings you could buy one bottle of Old London Gin, one bottle of Old Irish Whiskey, one bottle of Old Scotch Whiskey, one bottle of Martells Pale Brandy and a bottle of Old Jamaica Rum.

Christmas wreaths and crackers first appeared in the Monmouthshire Merlin of 1870. The first mention of a Christmas tree was around the 1870's. A C Norman was holding a Christmas raffle and was drawing attention to it with his Grand Christmas Tree. Tickets were a shilling each and prizes (displayed on the tree) would be distributed in time for them to be given as gifts at New Year.

Christmas being linked to children was becoming evident by now. In 1871 in the Monmouthshire Merlin, toys were described as being an 'indispensable part of Christmas'. A large and varied display could be seen at the shop of Mr F Martin, two doors away from the Town Hall in Newport as well as more costly items such as workboxes, writing desks, plated goods, bags etc. There were many articles also available for Christmas tree decorating.

Blands Bakery was steam powered by 1875, as well as being able to produce more bread and cakes, it was selling French confectionery, crystallized fruits and jellies.

Up until now most Christmas advertisements were appearing a few days before the event but in 1882,

London House in Newport was selling all sorts of goods for Christmas from the 4th of December.

In 1883, also in Newport, despite the weather being the 'reverse of seasonable', Christmas was kept with enthusiasm even though the atmosphere was damp and dull. Trade was brisk which enabled 'all classes, except the very poorest to indulge in festivity'. No small amount of artistic skill was shown in the decoration of establishments and this is how it continued. Christmas constantly grew in popularity and by the end of Queen Victoria's reign, Christmas advertisements in newspapers were almost filling whole pages and included toys such as rocking horses, building blocks, Noah's arks and trains.

By 1910 Newport was the place to be for Christmas shopping. The first Christmas shopping carnival was held in December of that year. The aim of the event was to bring to the attention of people the advantages of shopping in Newport. All the shops took part and the majority of them were specially decorated and where the weather would allow, the streets too. Lord Tredegar was due to open the event from the balcony of the Town Hall but due to other engagements was unable to do so. So, headed by trumpeters and mace bearers, the mayor in his robes and chains of office did the honours. A procession then walked to the market and judging took place for the best window dressing, market stall, decorations and illuminations. Later a luncheon was held at the Town Hall.

Christmas would never go back to the days of 1829. Nothing would stop Christmas, not even war.

CHARITY

In the early 19th century, and for many years before, the parish you lived in was responsible for giving you poor relief if you ever required it. Property owners paid a poor rate tax to provide grants of money, clothing, food and fuel to those in need. It was known as out relief, paid to the poor in their own homes.

The Poor Law Amendment Act aimed to end out relief for the able bodied pauper and at the same time save the parish money. This was achieved by the introduction of Poor Law Unions, central to which was the workhouse (though these had existed prior to this date). Poor relief was now only given to those desperate enough to enter the grim walls of these institutions.

Charity then, played a huge part in people's lives, especially at Christmas. For a large number of people winter would have been a very bleak time of year if not for the kindness shown by the more well off members of society. People such as Capel Hanbury Leigh of Pontypool who in December 1837

'caused the carcases of two fine bullocks, which had been slaughtered for the purpose, to be distributed amongst a large number of poor families and thus furnishing them with provision for a good Christmas dinner which many otherwise had not the means of procuring'.

The church also played a major part in the care and wellbeing of the poor. On Christmas Day in 1840 the whole of the poor of the parish of Penhow were given roast beef, plum pudding and ale by the Reverend J R Smith. In addition to this he, with his wife, had established a Sunday School attended by ninety children. They were also looking to establish a society to provide the poor with clothes.

Members of Parliament also provided for the poor. Still in 1840, on Christmas Day, the poor of Llantarnam were supplied by Mr Blewitt, with a substantial Christmas dinner of a pound of meat and a pound of bread for each individual in each family. He had begun this custom from his first year of residence at Llantarnam Abbey. He also provided the poor of the same parish with coal during the winter.

On the 26th December an article appeared in the Monmouthshire Merlin urging its readers to help the less well off of Newport. It gives a small glimpse as to just how desperate people were.

"Give coal and food – The weather is piercingly cold. Poverty, nay, destitution is at present the lot of many a hopeless family in the town and Pillgwenlly. The Christmas bright festival warms not their hearts, cheers not their desolate homes; but it smiles like moonbeams on the blasted heath, mocking sterility, making, as it were, their desolation more abjectly manifest".

Things were no better the following Christmas when the Merlin reported distress in general in the neighbourhood of Pontypool. The gift of beef was again delivered by Capel Hanbury Leigh with nearly two thousand pounds distributed to one thousand one hundred and forty individuals. A donation of thirty guineas was also given for a soup and potato fund for the town.

By the mid 1840's, the workhouses, whose aim had

been to deter the workshy, able bodied pauper from claiming poor relief, was housing the old, the sick, the disabled, single mothers and children. It was no doubt a grim existence for them however newspapers seem to suggest that at most Christmas times at least, they were well looked after.

In 1843, Madame Lee of the Priory, Caerleon distributed coal and articles of clothing suitable for the season. Children of the church Sunday school were among those who received items. Numbers attending had quadrupled during the year. Also Colonel Sir Digby Mackworth entertained a number of children, inmates of the Newport Union Workhouse and children belonging to the charity school, with tea and cake.

In other areas of the county, the Reverend Isaac Hughes, Curate of Mynyddislwyn had been enabled by Lady Hall of Llanover to distribute twenty pounds worth of flannel among the poor and Mr Davies of Abersychan Ironworks supplied all the poor widows of Varteg with a Christmas dinner of roast beef and plum pudding. Recipients numbered twenty three widows and their children.

There was no Christmas dinner for the poor in Newport Workhouse in 1845 though, as shown in a letter sent to the editor of the Monmouthshire Merlin.

"referring to a paragraph in your paper alluding to the objection of the district auditor to certain expenditure in this Union. I beg to say the Guardians found no fault with the auditor for his refusing to allow Christmas dinner to the paupers as he merely performed his duty in adhering to the instruction of Poor Law Commissioners whose opinion on the subject he produced. W D Evans, Clerk, Newport Union".

A reply was given by the editor.

"The paragraph referred to was sent to our office by a respectable correspondent who, though usually accurate, may have been misinformed. It is a fact however that dinner was refused".

The poor of Courtfield near Monmouth had a good Christmas in this year. A large quantity of clothing was distributed among them by John F Vaughn. Each family in the neighbourhood was supplied with Christmas dinner and Mrs Vaughn supplied each family with a quantity of coal which was hauled and left at each of their cottages.

In 1847, the Poor Law Commissioners relented and decided that pauper inmates of the workhouses could be fed differently on Christmas Day, as long as the Guardians saw fit. The Guardians of the Newport Workhouse ordered dinner of roast beef and plum pudding for all.

Charity continued, each and every year. Large estates such as Tredegar House, Malpas Court, The Firs and tradesmen of towns all cared for the distressed. In 1848 Capel Hanbury Leigh distributed flannel, coal, bread and soup among the poor while his wife gave large quantities of blankets,

The poor of the almshouses, usually older people were also looked after with charity. In 1867 the occupants of almshouses in Newport were presented, by the mayor, with a ton of coal each, in order to 'brighten the blaze of their Christmas fire'. Mr R F Woollet forwarded to them each, a shilling and a supply of beef and vegetables. Mr H P Bolt donated firewood. Mr GW Jones provided many of the poor in town with a Christmas dinner which he had been doing for ten years.

A fancy fair and gigantic Christmas tree was held in the British school room in Risca in 1870. The event was organised by the ladies of the neighbourhood for the purpose of adding to a fund towards the repairs of Risca church, the introduction of gas into the building and a new organ. The Christmas tree was a great attraction and amongst the stalls was needlework by Mrs Banks of Pontymister House, a refreshment stall run by Mrs Vaughn of the Ferns, a perfume stall run by Miss

Vaughn, a fortune telling stall managed by Miss Jenkins and a zoetrope by Miss Banks.

In Bassaleg, Lady Tredegar distributed blankets and warm clothes to about two hundred poor people besides which, about fifty were supplied weekly with broth, dripping and other offal from Tredegar House.

In 1874, in Risca, Mrs Heyworth carried on her yearly custom of supplying around forty old people with beef. Also Mrs Morris of Dan-y-graig and many others did not forget the poor. After service on Christmas Day the Reverend Hugh Williams gave some twenty old people bread and money.

Christmas Day dinner was given by Sir George Elliot to the inmates of Newport County infirmary in 1888. There were turkeys, game, plum puddings and desserts of all descriptions. In some instances men were allowed to smoke pipes of tobacco. The mayor was also present and the wards were decorated and thrown open to the public.

In Tredegar a dinner was given to two hundred and sixty children in Bedwelty workhouse. In the evening entertainment was given in the Union schools in the form of Mrs Jarley's waxworks. Mr Harris, Guardian for Nantyglo gave each child an orange and Mr and Mrs Peaty sent a quantity of Christmas cards.

An eisteddfod was held at the town hall, Blaenavon in connection with Ebenezer Baptist chapel. The Blaina choir won first prize of twelve pounds. A tea meeting was held in connection with King Street Baptist chapel and a sale of work in connection with Brunel Street chapel.

Problems struck in 1891 though, in Newport. The Christmas Cheer Fund which had been raised in the town for several years and out of which a large number of people were able to obtain a few luxuries at Christmas couldn't find anyone to oversee the collection.

But charity didn't end, by the twentieth century bigger projects and schemes to help the poor were being started. In December 1900, Dr. Rutherford Harris, M.P., decided to supply all the inmates of workhouses in Monmouthshire with Christmas books and pictures. This project was a result of a scheme by Mr W T Stead, editor of 'Reviews of Reviews', who wished to begin a project of the kind for all workhouses in Great Britain. Not knowing exactly who he should apply to, Mr Stead contacted Dr. Harris who, not only agreed to become the sponsor for Monmouthshire workhouses but for the whole of Wales.

Christmas and New Year Charities were in full preparatory swing in Newport in 1903. A meeting of a committee for the New Year treat for poor children was held at the Town Hall. It was decided to hold their fourteenth treat in the new year and aimed to provide hot dinners of roast beef and plum pudding, entertainment and bags of goodies for the children, estimated at three thousand five hundred. A prize of a watch would go to the person who could collect the most money.

The Newport Hot Pot Fund was also in its fourth year. In the previous year six hundred hot pots were distributed, each contained enough food to feed ten people for two days. The hot pot tins contained six hundred Christmas puddings, six hundred loaves of bread, packets of tea, joints of beef and groceries.

Free Christmas beer was phased out in 1903 as licensed victuallers opted to give the equivalent in money as a gift to local cottage hospital funds.

In 1904, the poor of Abergavenny, numbering around fifteen hundred, both adults and children, assembled at the market to receive from the hands of a committee, food consisting of a pound of beef for each adult, half a pound for each child, half a pound of plum pudding each and two pounds of potatoes each.

On Christmas Eve at the Market Hall in Abergavenny in 1915, around five hundred families, numbering around fifteen hundred adults and children were given a supply of food for a Christmas dinner - beef, potatoes, swede and plum pudding. The food was placed on a long tables so that the recipient could tell by referring to a letter on his ticket which table to go to. The letter 'A' represented one adult, 'B' one adult and one child, right up to 'M' which was for two adults and eleven children. The distribution was very orderly and most recipients had been supplied within twenty minutes.

SCHOOLS

The schools also closed for Christmas though it appears their holidays weren't quite as long as today's. An examination took place first though.

In 1832 at Newport Girls National school such an examination was held before Mrs Morgan of Ruperra and Sir Charles Morgan of Tredegar House. The appearance and improvement of the children was said to have given satisfaction. Sir Charles then distributed mince pies to all. A similar event took place at Newport British school.

Sir Charles, the founder of the institution gave these examinations regularly. In 1840 he was accompanied by a party from Tredegar House. It was reported in the Monmouthshire Merlin that the children were affectionately addressed by Sir Charles who was pleased with their progress. At the end of the examination some massive Christmas cakes which had been brought from Tredegar House were cut up and distributed to them.

In the Free Press of 1861 an article described the last day of term at Raglan National School and on the last day it was the annual custom of the vicar to give the children a treat. One hundred children met in the school room at two in the afternoon and continued to do so until three when the playing of games commenced. The game which seemed to be most in favour was that which required 'application of berries of the mistletoe and was interesting to note the phases of character in those men and women of the future'.

After three hours of play, the children were summoned by a roll call to take their places and enjoy a feast provided by the vicar's niece whose chief pleasure seemed to be to confer happiness on others. During the evening the children sang songs and at the close gave many cheers for the vicar and his niece and the ladies who had assisted.

The children had been issued tickets and on giving them to a superintendent, received sealed packets containing a sum of money. The school room was prettily decorated by the master, pupil teachers and elder scholars. There were festoons and wreaths of ivy, laurel and holly with mottoes printed in black, red and green and also various designs in chalk and crayon, one commemorating the death of the Prince Consort, another the Book of Truth and another with a dove of peace. All were surrounded by Yew, Mistletoe or Box and lighted up with chandeliers suspended from the ceiling. The children, after singing the national anthem were dismissed to their homes with cake, to return on the 30th of December.

Mrs Paton of Blaenavon visited the National Schools prior to breaking up for Christmas in 1865 and distributed books and treats among the children. She also distributed food among the poor families and widows of the ironworks.

Parents and former pupils were invited to Christmas events also as this letter to the Merlin on 22nd December 1876 shows.

(To the Editor of the Monmouthshire Merlin)

Dear Sir – The usual Christmas treat will be given in connection with this institution (Wesleyan Methodist

Sunday Ragged School) in the Temperance Hall on Tuesday 26th.

It is customary to invite the parents as well as the children to share in the pleasures of the school festival. This year the teachers have resolved to invite former scholars also – all of whom are above twenty years of age, and as far as practicable, secure their attendance and the presence of former teachers. A social meeting will be held in the same place after tea. A cordial welcome will be given to all who are desirous to attend. Short addresses will be delivered, presents distributed and the scholars will sing a variety of sacred pieces.

Kindly allow me through the Merlin to state that the teachers are collecting subscriptions to defray the expenses and it will contribute to our joy to receive this year again the support of Christian friends.

Yours obliged, Thomas Garrett, Superintendent, 37 Lewis Street.

The Church Sunday Schools at Pontymoile and Sebastopol held their annual prize giving meetings before breaking up for Christmas. At Sebastopol the children met their teachers and friends on the evening of 17th December 1879 and found in the school room a well stocked Christmas tree, the presents hanging on the branches provided by many in the community. The rector made a small speech giving encouragement to teachers and pupils and the prizes were distributed by Mrs Wailes, whose musical services in the parish were highly valued. The singing of hymns and recitations by the children added to the evening's enjoyment.

At Pontymoile prizes were distributed on the 20th by Mrs A A Williams. There was no Christmas tree but fun was had by searches in a bran tub. Each search brought up a present donated by the Rector and other members of the community. Several of the parents attended including Mr and Mrs W Mends of the G W Railway, the regular attendance and success of whose nine or ten children in the schools had been for some years a subject of congratulations.

CHRISTMAS EVE & CHRISTMAS MORNING

Christmas in Wales meant Plygain. A description of this early morning service was given by a contributor to the Monmouthshire Merlin in December 1838. It is also evident from the letter written by Hen Duaf, that he considered Plygain to be a dying custom.

"Plygain – not a more simple spectacle than a Welsh country church on Christmas morning, before dawn, when its plain gothic windows are seen illuminated by many lights, which with holly and evergreens have been carefully prepared the evening before and towards which may be seen proceeding, the old and the young, moving with their own candles which they have taken to add to the light in the church, but which if the morning is not illuminated by stars or moon, they kindle to light their path as they go, appearing as they move along like fireflies along fields and hedges.

The service performed by a Welsh curate in the midst of his rural flock, listening to the accents of religion in their ancient native language is a sight to be seen. I can only account for it being so little continued from the higher classes, considering sleep to be more important than going to church at an early hour. The hour is agreeable for the poor and service ends in time for the commencement of work. They always attend in large numbers before daily labour begins and for those whose masters allow a holiday, it is desirable they should be reminded of their duties before they begin their enjoyment or they might find it difficult to withdraw if called to church at ten or eleven o clock in the middle of preparations for the Christmas feast."

Another aspect of Plygain, was staying up during the early hours of Christmas morning until the church service, somewhere between three and six o clock. People might sit at home making toffee, play the harp and dance or in some areas spend the time playing in the streets. This appears to have happened in Monmouth in 1843 and people were not too happy about it.

"This (Christmas) festival was ushered in at Monmouth by the noisy portion of the inhabitants in a manner truly disgraceful. As the wearied with the restraints of the Sabbath, no sooner had the bells of St Mary's announced the return of the joyous day than these disorderly persons commenced parading through the streets. Shouts mingled with jests, knocking of doors mingled with the soft notes of the band and carols of the Primitive Methodists. The police were unable to keep the delinquents we have complained of in check who continue to disturb inhabitants til dawn."

This didn't stop the celebrations though and Christmas gatherings prevailed. In 1856 a supper party was held at the Fiddlers Arms, Abergavenny, when about eighty people attended. The food was provided by the landlord, Mr James Daniel and his wife. After toasts had been given, most of the guests retired to the dancing room where wives and children joined in various dances which continued to an early hour on Christmas morning.

Playing tricks seemed to have been common on

Christmas Eve as reported in Usk in 1856. During the night of the 24th, several tricks were played, two public lamps were broken and several carts were wheeled into the river. The Illustrated Usk Observer commented that the festive season rarely passed off in the town without 'mischief being done to property by worthless fellows'.

By 1864, partying in public houses until the early hours on Christmas morning appear to have been stopped. Some tried to keep their establishments open, but if caught they faced being fined. For example Henry Harris who was charged with keeping his house open at ten thirty at night on Christmas Eve. It was his third offence in the previous three months and P.C. 82 said he found sixteen men in the house drinking. He was fined thirty shillings.

In 1865, James Prosser of the Moon Inn, Cwmbran was charged with having his house open during prohibited hours. P.C. 53 stated he visited the house at six thirty on Christmas morning and after some delay the door was opened for him. On going in he thought he heard a noise in the cellar and asked for a light to go and see, when he was told that if he wanted a light he must get one. He went into the cellar and came in contact with a man's arm. He then struck a match and saw three men concealed. They had a jug with beer in it. The defendant was fined twenty shillings plus costs.

Plygain was still being observed in the second half of the century. In 1868 it took place in Abercarn, performed at five thirty in the morning by the Reverend David Charles in Lord Llanover's church. A sermon was preached, in Welsh to an overflowing congregation. The church was decorated with evergreens and brilliantly lighted.

Similarly, plygain took place in Llanover where the Reverend Evan Bevan preached to a numerous congregation. The church was decorated with evergreens and well lighted with candles brought by many of the congregation.

In Bassaleg, the school children, around one hundred and twenty were entertained by Lady Tredegar at Tredegar Park with tea and cake, Lady Tredegar having attended the school the day before for the children's examination and reward of books.

Similar services were held the following year however in 1871 in Ebbw Vale, Christmas was a much more solemn affair due to an outbreak of smallpox. In the five weeks prior to Christmas, around one hundred people had died from Smallpox and other diseases. It was said a hospital was greatly needed for the place was not as sanitary as it should have been. There was no sounds of music or anything in the streets

By contrast, in Blaenavon, the weather was wet and foggy but evidence of Christmas was everywhere. Long before daybreak the church bells rang out and carol singers were heard in all directions. All unnecessary work was suspended and services were held in churches decorated in evergreens.

The decoration of churches for Christmas was described in the Western Mail in 1871. The church concerned was St Mary's in Chepstow whose decorations were deemed more elegant than of previous years. In front of the organ gallery was text on a white background on which was illuminated the words 'let everything that hath breath praise the Lord'. Along the two side galleries was a specimen of the ladies handiwork in cotton, wool, evergreens and berries surmounted by a large cross. The font was decorated with a pyramid made of flowers and evergreens surmounted with a cross. The reading desk was all covered with evergreens, holly and berries. The arches of the nave and chancel were festooned with wreaths of evergreens and on the walls, several garlands hung. All services were largely attended.

Lower Cwmbran was the scene of conflict on Christmas Eve in 1873. Two young men, maddened by drink, had a row and proceeded to settle their dispute with a fight. The father of one, a puddler named Powell, tried to part them but was stabbed in the chest by his son's opponent. He was charged and remanded.

Lord Llanover's church in Abercarn was once more the scene of plygain in 1880. The church was overflowing and Reverend G Watson officiated and preached a Welsh sermon. The building was decorated with sprigs of holly and ivy. The arches and gothic windows bordered with the same.

Carol singers were out on Christmas Eve in Newport in 1883. Also several bands playing music were out as well. As midnight struck, the bells of St Woollos notified the dawn of another Christmas Day.

By the end of the century, Christmas trees had become popular. They were usually present at charity events, laden with gifts that were either raffled off or presented to children. On Christmas Eve in 1892 in Blaenavon, the King's Baptists held a tea meeting in their school room. They had a Christmas tree and sale of useful ornamental articles. A magic lantern drew in large numbers of young people. After Christmas the school room had to be opened again to clear up numerous articles not disposed of.

Horeb Baptist Chapel choir gave a successful cantata entitled 'The Night of Glory' in 1892. The duets, quartets and choruses were greatly admired. The choir had been under the training of Mr B Jones. A pianoforte solo by Miss M A Evans was played with 'much taste'. The accompanist during the evening was Miss Polly Scourfield. Mr Padfield played the organ. The chapel was more than half full but when considering the attractions elsewhere this was deemed very good.

A dense fog prevailed in Brynmawr, nevertheless many people were out on the streets. At seven p.m., when Mr J Vowell's brass band was playing in King Street, a trap with two female occupants drove up. The horse took fright and scattered the musicians damaging their instruments to the value of twelve pounds. The owner, Mrs Pritchard of Llanvihangle near Abergavenny was in the vehicle and was thrown in the road sustaining serious injuries. During the confusion which followed, the animal broke the shafts and bolted in the direction of Llanelly where it was captured.

CHRISTMAS DAY

An early Christmas Day story concerns Abergavenny Castle in the year 1175. It had been established around the year 1087 by Lord Hamelin de Ballon during a time of fighting between the Normans and the Welsh. In 1172, a Welsh chieftain, Systyllt ap Dyferwald captured the castle but it was soon recaptured by the Normans. In the 1160's, Henry Fitzmiles, son of de Ballon, was killed fighting Systyllt. As there was now no male heir with Henry's death, the castle passed to the husband of one of de Ballon's daughters, William de Braose.

In 1175, William de Braose invited Systyllt, his son Geoffrey and other leading Welsh chieftains to the castle in what appeared to be an effort to bring about peace. A feast was held on Christmas Day in the Great Hall but on arrival, the hall doors were locked and Systyllt and his party were massacred.

Moving forward to the nineteenth century and it is generally accepted that Queen Victoria's husband Prince Albert introduced the Christmas tree to Britain in the 1840s. However, a letter to the Monmouthshire Merlin in the year 1830, suggests the county had its own tree already.

"Sir" wrote Viator, from Caerleon, "my paternal mansion is situated in a small parish on the road between Newport and Pontypool.

I remember in my earliest infancy that some of the inhabitants of the village were accustomed at or about Christmas Day to present at the door a humble offering of the following description for which they generally received, from my father, a handsome bounty. To each of the branches of a slightly made wooden tree, resembling the shape and appearance, though not in size, one of those ancient pieces of furniture found in some houses for guests to hang their hats upon, was fixed an apple. Every apple was stuck full of oaten grains and to each of the grains was attached a small raisin, the whole tree being ornamented around with sprigs of holly.

Having been absent from the country for more than twenty years, I find on my return that most of the old parishioners are gone to their long homes and with them all trace of this wonderful tree"

As well as printing reader's memories of Christmases past, local papers also recorded how it was being celebrated in the present. In 1842, members of the Total Abstinence Society, Monmouth, celebrated Christmas by having a tea party and dance in the market hall. Around four hundred people attended. The party ended at midnight with the people delighted with the evening's amusements.

In 1848, the inmates of the Abergavenny workhouse, though not clothed in their usual purple, received roast beef and plum pudding and cwrw da. Mr Bevan, the master, it was reported in the Monmouthshire Merlin 'always beams with kindness towards the poor, many of whom had seen, if not days of affluence, those of comfort. He tends to provide for them, at least once a year, a kind of good living, to try to ease from their mind that they are paupers'. Mr Bevan had collected in town £12 towards this Christmas feast. There was about ninety poor people who attended, the men were able to sit 'behind their yard of clay' while the old women preferred snuff. There was enough money left over to provide them with another celebratory meal on New Year's Day. The seventy five bedridden inmates had their meals in their rooms.

However, writers at the Monmouthshire Merlin were not impressed with Christmas in Pontypool in 1848.

"We do not recall a more dull Christmas in Pontypool. In consequence of depression of trade which is severely felt by the tradesmen. The public houses were thinly attended, not as in former times when Christmas Day was similar to a fair in comparison of numbers. The superintendent of police gave notice to publicans that the same rules would be enforced on Christmas Day as on the Sabbath which proved so effectual that parties were enabled to attend their place of worship without being annoyed by drunken brawlers".

Our ancestors, just as we do today, hoped for a white Christmas, though they didn't always get them. The weather appears to have been just as unpredictable at Christmas then, as it is now. In 1849, Christmas Day in Monmouthshire was fine and bracing but it then became humid and overcast with sleet and hail after which a severe frost set in with biting north winds. The day was observed as a holiday in Newport by a large majority of tradesmen which gave their assistants an opportunity to visit friends. A few shops opened though, in opposition to the general wish of the inhabitants St Woollos church was decorated with emblems of Christmas and a full service was performed by the choir. Two anthems were also sung in the morning and two in the evening.

The eisteddfod was popular as a Christmas entertainment. In 1854 the reverend J E Jones of Ebbw Vale carried off fifteen prizes for different essays and poems at the Christmas Eisteddfod. Churches and chapels were attended by most people and were places to meet socially as well as worship. In 1855 in Abergavenny, a social tea meeting was held on Christmas Day at the Baptist chapel, Lion Street when about two hundred people attended. There were addresses on a variety of topics. The Reverend Mr Poole spoke about the pleasures and advantages of true religion. Mr Roberts spoke abut the benefits of holding tea meetings and Mr Morgan, on Peace

Christmas was much more communal in Victorian times, for example employers providing Christmas dinner for employees and their families and many of the following accounts reflect this.

In 1856, Christmas dinner of roast beef and plum pudding was prepared at Herefordshire House, Frogmore Street, Abergavenny, on Christmas Day by Mr and Mrs Jenks for the employees of Mr James Morgan, coach proprietor, paid for by him. All his servant men were invited. About twenty were present during which Mr Morgan paid them a visit and addressed them in a 'gentlemanly manner'. He said he was perfectly happy with their past conduct and he hoped they would enjoy the evening and hoped to meet them all again at the end of the year. After applause for Mr Morgan, he left and the evening was spent in a cordial manner with songs and toasts. As the men dispersed they said they had spent the happiest evening of their lives.

In 1857, in Blaenavon, the church choir was entertained at T W Plum's with an 'excellent supper'. During the evening several choruses, trios, duets and solos were performed by the choir. After supper, the health of Mr Plum and his family was drunk. At the conclusion, one of the choir returned thanks to the host and hostess for their kind treat.

At Llanarth, the tradesmen and labourers on Llanarth Estate sat down to a 'substantial dinner of English fare' given by Mrs Herbert who also distributed a quantity of

Welsh flannel to the poor.

The Union workhouse in Monmouth had a gala day at Christmas in 1859. The inmates were given Christmas dinner and later in the day took part in various kinds of amusements. The governor and matron, Mr and Mrs Rogers, who it was said, took so much interest in the welfare of the poor under their care were highly spoken of by the Guardians and the paupers. They prepared two large Christmas trees upon which were several hundred prizes. Great fun was had in the drawing of lots for the prizes which were sometimes unsuitable for the owners.

At Llanarth Court in 1859, work people and farm labourers on the estate of J Arthur Herbert, about fifty, sat down to dinner in the servants hall of the mansion which was decorated with holly and mistletoe. Several Welsh and Irish mottoes were placed in vases on the table, also a variety of fruits, the drink being lemonade. After toasts to the health of Mr and Mrs Herbert, songs were sung and concluded with old Father Christmas performing on the terrace.

Elsewhere, in Newport, all the shops were closed and peals poured from the bells of St Woollos. A couple of drum and fife bands paraded the streets. There was very little entertainment open to the public. The absence of drunkenness was noted and no cases were brought before the magistrates. Praise was given in the Monmouthshire Merlin to the temperance societies whose efforts had contributed to the results.

Inmates of the Pontypool Union workhouse were treated to Christmas dinner of roast beef and plum pudding in 1860 and the Monmouthshire Merlin reported that it was pleasing to hear from impartial and disinterested sources that the inmates were treated in a kind manner at all times by the master and matron Mr and Mrs Protheroe.

In 1861, the Monmouth Grand Amateur Music Festival was held at Christmas. There was upward of forty performers of the Monmouth Philharmonic and Vocal Association together with the Usk Madrigal Society. Captain Carter performed on the flute and Miss Bessie Waugh, a talented townswoman, on pianoforte. Mr Perry, bandmaster of the Monmouthshire Militia led the instrumentals. The audience was said to have been disappointed by the absence of James Nash who was announced in the posters

.An eisteddfod was held at Penuiel Methodist chapel in Blaenavon in 1862. A large number of prizes, mostly useful books were given for the best singing and reciting in English and Welsh. The first meeting began at 10.30 am, chaired by Mr John Lewis, furnace manager. The afternoon and evening meetings by Mr Joseph Kay. The morning attendance was not very large but many attended the others.

In Beaufort, the British room was decorated for the eisteddfod and a hundred competitors had sent in their names. A lively meeting was expected.

Mr James of Uskside Ironworks gave a tea party to the wives and children of his workmen in 1863. It was also open to as many of the men who wanted to attend. About a hundred and fifty of all ages were present. The tables were laid with home made cake and bread and butter. Mr James opened a dance by leading out Mrs Ovens to the sound of a fiddle. The evening passed with great hilarity with two workmen dressed as Punch and Judy. A prize was given to the tenant's wife who kept the cleanest cottage, which was Mrs Ovens. Dancing continued until midnight.

About a hundred old people, inhabitants of Pillgwenlly were entertained at a dinner provided for them in the Temple Street schoolroom. The expenses were covered by a subscription among members and congregation of Trinity Church. After dinner addresses were given by Reverend Fox.

The annual shooting of geese and hares took place at

the range of the third Monmouthshire Volunteer Corps in Newport in 1866 when a number of volunteers were present.

The children and parents of the Wesleyan Methodist Sunday Ragged School, Dock Street, Newport were invited to a Christmas tea in 1867. The selection of food provided included goose, cake, oranges, nuts and tea. After tea, singing took place and reward books were distributed for good conduct.

The Christmas weather in Pontypool in 1869 was not very seasonal. The 23rd saw a violent thunderstorm while on Christmas Day the sky was almost cloudless until drenching showers returned.

After plygain, a second church service was held around mid morning. This took place in English and in Llanover in 1869 was at eleven o clock. After church the annual Christmas dinner was given to around two hundred tenants and workmen of Lady Llanover. Welsh grace was sung before and after dinner and also a Welsh harp was played. At five in the afternoon dancing began which did not end until ten. There was plenty of Christmas fare and desserts to hand though drinking was on temperance principles.

Christmas at Llanover was described in a little more detail in the Monmouthshire Merlin the following year. Because Christmas Day fell on a Sunday, the annual dinner was on Monday when one hundred and fifty people sat down to tables covered with roast beef, mutton, pork, plum pudding, mince pies, fruit pies but no alcohol. Welsh grace was sung before and after dinner and the health of Lady Llanover was proposed, also in Welsh. The Reverend Evan Bevan gave a Welsh address and prizes were awarded by Lady Llanover to tenant farmers for the best flocks of sheep, the best turnips, best white washed cottage and best garden. All the prizes were money in purses with clasps suspended to ribbons. Lady Llanover addressed each recipient in Welsh. After prize giving, the evening consisted of Welsh songs, poetry and dance until ten o clock when all went home.

The poor of Caerleon were invited to Christmas dinner by Mr and Mrs R Graham of the Red Lion Inn in 1874. They had the usual meal of roast beef and plum pudding and their appreciation of such a charitable act showed in repeated rounds of cheers.

'Real old Christmas weather' was reported in Pontypool in this year. The landscape was covered in snow, the canals and ponds were covered in ice and preparations were everywhere for the observance of the festival. Churches were decorated and St Albans was mentioned for its elaborate and artistic style. The Guardians of the workhouse were determined the poor should have a good dinner and the Hanbury or 5th Monmouthshire Riflemen also held a Christmas dinner.

Newspapers reported Christmas Day passing quietly in Pontypool in 1875. Services were held at several places of worship in the morning and in the evening. There was a tea party at Mount Pleasant chapel and it was noted that at Trevethin church the usual amount of decoration was not displayed due to its being painted inside. St James's church on the other hand produced a 'nice effect' by Mrs Bunning, the Misses Williams of High Street, Reverend J D Lewis and Reverend Rees. Inscriptions were painted in white on scarlet backgrounds with borders of evergreens. Those in the chancel had blue backgrounds. Over the East window was placed a large monogram and cross in gold, blue and crimson on a white background. At St Albans the walls were decorated with banners, pictures and laurel leaves in heart shapes with ivy leaves looped up between them.

It was also reported that Christmas in Abergavenny had not been quite so lively, neither had the shops presented a seasonable appearance. St Mary's church however was 'beautifully decorated with evergreens and an artistically devised text'. Services were held in the churches and chapels and all the shops were shut. A number of people went out with the 'harriers' and enjoyed some sport.

The Pontypool Battalion of the 1st Monmouthshire Artillery Volunteers took part in a Christmas prize shooting at Cwmlickey range. There were a number of prizes to compete for. The mountain was covered in snow and the cold was intense but they had a good time, lit a fire and took their own refreshments. The prizes were awarded in the evening at the Winning Horse Hotel.

Christmas decorations were of course popular but very different to how we decorate today. The emphasis was on making your own and gathering what nature provided.

In 1876 Lady Llanover entertained her tenants at her home yet again. The Cambrian newspaper described the scene. On entering the servants hall, opposite the door was a large banner hanging on the wall with the words 'Long life to Lady Llanover' in white letters on a scarlet background. Above the entrance was a banner with a leek and the words 'Tywysograeth Cymru'. The tables, covered in food were decorated with ferns and evergreens, in the midst of which were mini banners. At one thirty, dinner was served to the assembled tenants and afterwards the tables were cleared and speeches given by Mr Phineas James (agent), Reverend Bevan (domestic chaplain) until almost five o clock. Songs were also sung.

Tea was then served, in another room, while the hall was cleared for dancing. After tea, the guests returned where, accompanied by 'Gruffydd' (harpist to the Prince of Wales) on the triple harp they danced to a late hour.

The master of Newport workhouse, Mr Needham, reported in 1876, that the inmates returned thanks for their Christmas dinner. The Christmas tree, provided by Mrs Cartwright was greatly admired. Several copies of 'The Graphic' were presented to the inmates by Mrs Lovell. The vice chairman gave oranges and apples to the children. Mrs Ward presented several dolls and illustrated books also for the children and Mr Norman, station master, presented a large parcel of illustrated papers.

Children went carol singing on Christmas Day though sometimes it didn't end well. At the County petty sessions before Lord Tredegar in 1876, Henry Day, aged twelve and William aged ten were charged with stealing a thermometer, the property of Mr Batchelor. On Christmas Day they went to his house to sing and after they had left the thermometer was missed. When caught the boys blamed each other and said they had broken it and thrown it into Mr Earl's garden, where it was found. The charges were not pressed but a fine of five shillings was imposed.

A Christmas tree was held at the Drill Hall in Blackwood in 1880 and was well attended. The tree was decorated with useful and fancy articles provided by the ladies of the neighbourhood. During the afternoon and the evening a programme of music and singing was given. The proceeds were in aid of St Margaret's church.

In Risca on Christmas night in 1881, entertainment was given in Bethany Baptist chapel. Songs and recitations were given by teachers of the Sunday School. A dialogue 'The Bachelors Club' was recited by seven young men with proceeds going to the Sunday School.

As the century went on, the poor were still not overlooked and in 1883 Christmas dinner was served at many establishments. At the industrial schools the children were presented with toys.

Tuesday the 25th December in 1883 was not a typical Christmas Day according to the Western Mail. There was no frost or snow so a damper was put on all outdoor sports and festivities, especially with the added arrival of a dense and depressing fog. Church and chapel services took place though, again many decorated with evergreens, flowers and text and including tea meetings and Eisteddfodau.

The Weekly Mail recorded in 1887 that there had been a taste of the seasonable Christmas of days gone by. A bit of a thaw had set in on Christmas Eve but Christmas Day was bright and clear with a dry frosty atmosphere. In the evening a sharp frost set in but changed to sudden pouring rain which ended with a heavy fall of snow.

Christmas Day passed in a very dull manner in Chepstow, said the South Wales Daily News in 1888. A misty rain had been falling all day. The inmates of the workhouse were treated to Christmas dinner in the large dining hall and the parish church was decorated, with a carol service held at night. The annual tea and entertainment took place at the British school with singing by friends of various chapels. Beginning at seven in the evening a large crowd attended.

By the 1890's 'quiet' was a word being used to describe Christmas more and more. In 1891, the Western Mail said that there was little of a public character in Newport on Christmas Day to engage attention beyond the church services. The weather had been cold all week and skating at Alexandra Dock and other sheets of ice in the neighbourhood had taken place. There was a slight shower but instead of bringing about a thaw the frost became more intense and soon the streets were covered in sheets of ice. There was scarcely any transport, the trams and buses to Maindee ran for a portion of the day. Rail traffic though was very heavy and outstripped the record of any year.

It was pretty much the same in 1893 in Pontypool. The papers stated only slight reference needed to be made towards the celebrations of Christmas. There were services in the churches and non conformist places of worship. Inmates had their usual Christmas dinner. In the evening various entertainments were to be found all given in places of worship. At the Undenominational Mission Hall in Pontymoile, Mr Tim Wintle gave a lecture describing the origin of the mission which had been in existence for about eighteen years and had been instrumental in accomplishing great good.

In Blaenavon the weather was fine and frosty and skating had been enjoyed at Keepers Pond.

Christmas in Newport passed quietly, the day was fine but showers fell in the evening. There were services at most of the established churches and free churches. The inmates of the workhouse and those at Caerleon schools had extra fayre and the old people in the almshouses were given gifts. There was little drunkenness in town, the streets were busy from an early hour. Thousands of train passengers arrived for a football match between Usk Siders and Northumberland. The crowd was around twelve thousand. The Empire and Victoria theatres were well patronized as were the public houses.

It was a similar story in 1898 in Pontypool. Mr and Mrs Richards were the master and matron of the workhouse assisted by other officers who gave the usual meal to the inmates. The infirmary also was decorated by Nurse Anderson and her assistants, the patients being made as comfortable as their circumstances would permit.

Into the twentieth century and in Abergavenny in 1901, through the generosity of the public, the vicars and churchwardens were able to distribute over five hundred hot dinners to the poor on Christmas Day. Dinners were served at Mr Evan Jones's Imperial Coffee Tavern and consisted of roast beef and plum pudding.

"A green Christmas makes a fat churchyard" said the Weekly Mail in 1901 and so its prediction for the next quarter's health returns was poor. Frosty conditions had promised to make Christmas Day an ice bound skating day but a series of heavy downpours made it an indoor festival with the streets being in a very slushy state.

After a quiet Christmas Eve, people flocked into the streets of a chilly and damp Newport in 1902. It was reported the work of the post office was greater than ever with parcel traffic twenty five per cent higher than the previous year and there was a large increase in Christmas cards. A hot pot distribution took place and at the workhouse, the master, Captain Evan Davies supplied Christmas dinner in a decorated dining room. Men who smoked were given two ounces of tobacco, the women, four ounces of tea and a pound of sugar. Each was also given a pound of cake and four oranges. At night entertainment was provided by Colonel Wallis.

The annual Christmas tree and entertainment was held at Newport and Monmouthshire Hospital in 1903. It was attended by a large number of patients, nurses and staff as well as townspeople. A huge tree, twelve feet in height, donated by Lord Tredegar was set up in the children's wards and was covered in all kinds of toys and sweets. Dr. Fiddian, the house surgeon played Father Christmas. Matron served tea to visitors and later entertainment was given in number one ward.

Similarly, at Newport Sanatorium, Allt yr yn, the wards were decorated and a crowd gathered to witness the annual Christmas tree and distribution of toys. The presentation took place in a ward of the new pavilion allotted to scarlet fever cases. Lord Tredegar donated the tree and the toys were subscribed for by a large number of former patients.

Newport and Monmouthshire Hospital held its annual Christmas Tree and distribution of presents again in 1908. The children's ward was turned into fairyland with a huge tree donated by Lord Tredegar that reached from floor to ceiling. It was illuminated with coloured electric lamps and filled with presents and toys. Snow had fallen heavily outside and was represented inside by bobs of cotton wool hanging from the ceiling. Dr H Oakley, senior house surgeon was Santa, in a red cloak with white fur and white flowing beard. He handed presents from the tree to the patients. The Eleanor ward, reserved for women, represented a Japanese village, the patients in Eastern gowns which they had made themselves. A concert was given in the evening which included songs, recitations and piano and violin solos.

In 1910, Christmas was celebrated in Abergavenny with a friendly game against Llanfoist.

WORK

Not everyone had a day off at Christmas, many establishments did their best trade on a Christmas Day. The public houses were open, the police were working, doctors were working, and many other professions.

In 1840 in Newport, Mr Bowen of the Ship and Launch had cause to call the police. Samuel Parsons, a 'hungry looking sinner with red hair' as the Monmouthshire Merlin described him, was caught trying to steal a leg of mutton on Christmas night. Parsons was regarded as a 'greedy man' who had wandered in and grabbed the meat and was about to make off with it, when a bell close by rang. A woman called Sarah Green ran out and saw him with the mutton. Mr Bowen was then sent for and Parsons was delivered into the custody of Superintendent Hoskins. Parsons pleaded that the leg of mutton had met him in the passage as he was entering 'just fer summut to drink'. He was taking it back to the kitchen when he was charged with robbery. He was committed to trial at the next Sessions.

In the same year William Williams was charged with assaulting P.C. Harlow at the Hare and Greyhounds in

Newport on Christmas Eve. The prisoner was asked how many times he had been in jail to which he replied

"Why, I don't know, I'm sure; maybe once or twice p'raps"

Mr Hopkins stated he had visited Usk Gaol once every Christmas for the past seven years, as well as summer visits. He was fined ten shillings.

In Blaenavon, in 1860, William Roberts was charged in the police court with having stolen a piece of meat and three noggins of rum on Christmas Eve, the property of Rees Jones. Mr Jones had purchased the meat at Abergavenny and on going to take it from the porter stores where he had temporarily left it, he missed a bottle containing the noggins of rum. While looking for the rum, he missed the meat. P. C. Cook, traced Roberts to Blaenavon where he found him in bed at about eight thirty in the morning on Christmas Day. He then charged him and on going downstairs, P. C. Cook asked a female who was present for the meat. She produced it as asked, wrapped in a handkerchief. On asking for the rum though, she said she and Roberts had drunk it. Roberts said he had taken the meat by mistake and the rum had been given to him but he eventually pleaded guilty and was sent to the House of Correction for three months.

An inquest was held at the Kings Arms Inn, Blaenavon on Christmas Day 1863 before Edgar Batt, coroner, on the body of D Lloyd, collier. Joseph Richards, a haulier was a witness and said he was employed at Dodd's Slope. At eleven in the morning of the twenty first of December, he took a tram to Lloyd's stall. He went to fetch it back at three thirty in the afternoon when he found Lloyd lying with his neck on the crossbar of the tram. He was dead. He also said he found Lloyd having fits on many occasions. The verdict was that Lloyd died from suffocation.

Landlords of public houses were often in danger of working the wrong hours! In 1866, John Harris of the

Tilers Arms, Blaina was summoned for having his premises open during prohibited hours – quarter past five in the afternoon on Christmas Day.

There were times when people became annoyed that they couldn't work at Christmas.. In 1869 the editor of the Monmouthshire Merlin received a letter from such a person.

"Why were the plate layers belonging to some districts on the South Wales railway prevented to work on Christmas Day and the following day, while men in other districts were allowed to work and receive full pay? And, as ten shillings is a considerable amount to a family, a reply through some medium, from the authorities would greatly oblige the men who feel they have been unjustly treated"

Dr. Mullingham of Talywain was on call in 1880. A little girl, the daughter of John Moore swallowed a half penny on Christmas Day and almost all hope for her life was given up on. Her mother took her to Dr. Mullingham and he managed to get the bronze coin out of her stomach. It was lying flatways. The child then progressed well.

The afternoon of Christmas Eve 1883 brought a scene in St Mary's Street, Chepstow. A gentleman in clerical dress was walking along the pavement near Mr Thomas's grocery shop, perhaps on his way to church to take the evening service, when a well dressed youth of sturdy build, armed with a horse whip went up to him and gave him a thrashing. The recipient had a walking stick but didn't use it but ran away down the street to laughter from spectators. The youth assaulted him because one of his sisters had been annoyed by unwanted attentions from the clerical man and law proceedings were going to follow.

Popular cantata 'Christmas at School' was performed at Upper Trosnant Chapel, Pontypool, on Christmas night under the leadership of Mr B George. There was a large audience despite other attractions and the performance was very successful.

An entertainment was given on Christmas night in the Tabernacle Chapel under the presidency of the pastor. All participants were well applauded by the audience.

A lone hairdresser refused to close his shop in George Street Pontypool in 1891. This annoyed a passer by so much he complained to the Pontypool Free Press -

'the chairman of the Hairdressers Union refused to close, although it being a Bank Holiday and knowing very well that there were several assistants wishing to get home for Christmas and unable to get back until late on Saturday. If all had closed on Saturday it certainly would have been a great benefit to both assistants and masters and I really think it a shame that the chairman of the Union should be the only one to refuse, thus causing all of them to be open and depriving the assistants of their Christmas holidays. Allan'

A riot took place in Pontymister on Christmas Day 1893. At three o clock in the afternoon, soon after the pubs had closed, a crowd of around two hundred people assembled on the bridge at the entrance to the works and asked Superintendent Bosanquet for permission to go inside and have a discussion with the free labourers inside. He refused and the men adopted a more defiant attitude and demanded to be let in. About forty police were guarding the entrance. There had been a long dispute between the firm and the workmen. The local workers had been locked out of the steelworks and free labour had been brought in from elsewhere. The families affected by this received no financial help from Union strike pay as they were locked out and not actually on strike. The riot was an attempt to remove the free labourers and get their jobs back.

The men therefore threatened to break through and enter the works anyway. Superintendent Bosanquet appealed to them to be calm and return home but they refused. The superintendent was then struck in the face with a missile which cut his lip so he gave the order for the police to charge. The constables drew their batons and rushed at the crowd. A number of men were struck by the police and some were seriously injured. Superintendent Bosanquet then sent a message to Newport for extra police and for military help. Later about fifty men of the forty first Welsh regiment proceeded to Pontymister. Once there they entered the works and stayed overnight. Several of the rioters were tried in court and received various sentences but were eventually released by order of the Home Secretary.

BOXING DAY

It is said Boxing Day may date back to the middle ages. A theory is that it was named after priests opening the alms boxes that held donations to the poor. The Evening Express of 1907 said of the day that it was a custom for apprentices to carry around a money box to their master's customers asking for small donations for themselves. The day chosen for this was the day after Christmas and so became known as Boxing Day.

It is also known as St Stephens day or the Feast of Stephen. It was St Stephen's day that was being celebrated in 1849 at the Carpenters Arms in Newport. A supper was held by Stephen and William Iggulden who laid before a large gathering a 'sumptuous' feast.

The Monmouthshire Merlin had some thoughts about Boxing Day in 1855.

"Then comes the great, the eventful day to the poorer classes, called Boxing Day, which is now divested of much of that real kindness and neighbourly feeling which used to attend the gifts called Christmas boxes; they are now too often given merely to get rid of a troublesome beggar, for seldom are they given with any other feeling; and, on the other hand, it but too frequently happens that the money is spent by those who receive it in low extravagance and debauchery"

By 1874, Boxing Day was being kept as a holiday and a day for sporting activities and other entertainment. The annual competition for Christmas fare took place on the

Marshes by the members of the seventh Monmouthshire Rifle Volunteers. The conditions were five rounds at two hundred yards and an entrance fee of one shilling and sixpence was charged. Fifty nine volunteers entered. The prizes were given by Captain-Commandant Wyndham Jones and the officers of the corps. There were many high scores and every competitor received a prize. These were distributed at the drill hall in the evening.

Private John Trew won a ton of coal. Captain O. Goss, a pair of Highland shooting boots. Private. Pitt, a turkey. Corporal E. Wangler, a silk hat. Sergeant Williams, Private Stockwell, Colour Sergeant Francis, Private Grove and Sergeant J Williams all won turkeys. Colour Sergeant Mayo, pheasants and a bottle of sherry. Private Macey, a goose. Private Thomas, a cask of beer. Private Barton, a leg of pork. Private Hilton, a hare. Private Bruce, a fowl. Private Senior, a bottle of port. Private Wood, a bottle of brandy and Private Thorn, a brace of rabbits.

In 1875, Edmund Davies and James Oram were charged with boxing on Boxing Day. They both pleaded guilty to a breach of the peace after fighting in a field at Pentrepeod. They were fined ten shillings each.

The Royal Albert Hall, Newport held a grand concert on the afternoon of Boxing Day, 1877. Several eminent vocalists and musicians were engaged for the occasion including Eos Moorlais, Miss Griffiths, Dr. Frost and Mr Owen Williams. People who wished to procure a few hours entertainment were advised to buy tickets for this event.

In 1879 the First Monmouthshire Rifle Volunteers of Chepstow held their Christmas shooting. Prizes though, said the South Wales Daily News, were not so numerous nor of such value as in former years and as a result only twenty three competitors entered. The main prizes were won by Corporal Marmont and Privates T Johnson, H Bailey and W Fisher.

Boxing Day was a washout in 1880, rain fell steadily

throughout the day and at times poured down. However this did not deter the meeting of Lord Tredegar's fox hounds which took place at ten thirty in the morning at Ebbw bridge. Hundreds of people turned out despite the weather and by the time the hounds threw off, a large field had gathered on horseback and on foot. Many ladies attended and a number of the men wore pink. The fox ran at a fast pace and the hunt ran across country for fifty minutes before the fox got into an open drain and escaped. The 'brush' was not secured as a trophy but the day was enjoyed by those who attended.

The annual dinner to the workmen of the Pontypool Gas and Water Company took place at the manager's house on Boxing Day evening 1886. There was plenty of festive food and many songs were sung. The principal singers were Messrs Lloyd, Jones, Pitman, Harris and Johnson. After singing 'God Save the Queen' the party broke up about ten o clock.

In 1888 in the Western Mail it was reported that the success of Boxing Day in Newport was marred by wet weather. Business was suspended and townspeople enjoyed what entertainment was on offer. There was a football match with the Maoris in the afternoon which attracted a large crowd even though the ground was wet.

For those who didn't like football, there were two grand performances of Dr. Parry's opera 'Blodwyn' and special trains were running up and down the valleys for these events.

In Monmouth, Boxing Day was also kept as a holiday. There was no lack of entertainment for those who spent the day in town. There was a pigeon shooting match at the Royal Oak and rabbit coarsing at Manson's Cross. At the Rolls Hall, Mr Hermann's performance of Uncle Tom's Cabin was well attended.

A successful bazaar was held in Griffithstown in the schoolroom of the Baptist Chapel. The various stalls were tastefully arranged and decorated, the museum and art gallery forming an important attraction. The bazaar was opened by Mr I Butler, J.P. who said that it always gave him pleasure to help those who were helping themselves.

William Selby was summoned for being drunk and riotous in Maesycwmmer in 1891. He pleaded guilty adding that 'it being Boxing Day and all, he had a drop too much'. P. C. Watkins said that at 8 p.m on the 26th Selby was very drunk and was using very bad language on the highway near the Junction Inn, Maesycwmmer. He refused to give his name and address which had to be got from his landlord. Selby repeated his plea as to the holiday, the Magistrates Clerk asked him if he was bound to get drunk because it was a holiday. Selby replied that he did not often get drunk but he usually took a drop too much after Christmas. He was fined seven shillings.

The Abercarn v Lydbrook match was well attended in 1891 despite the bad weather, torrential rain. The Pontypool Free Press regarded it as an interesting game but not very noteworthy in the first half.

The Grand Eisteddfod in Abersychan however was much more successful and it was thought it might become an annual fixture. Mr W Lewis of Glansychan House was the president and Mr T Thomas of Newbridge the conductor. The adjudicators were – Music, Mr C Videon Harding. Recitations Dr Edwards of Pontypool College. Knitting, Mrs W Lewis and timbering, Mr J Brace.

The annual sale of work in connection with the Baptist Chapel of Forgeside, Blaenavon took place in 1892 and was opened by Mrs Danks. The children's fruit stall was well patronised and considering the weather a good amount of business was carried out. At intervals there were magic lantern performances during the evening.

William Jones was charged with being drunk at Blaenavon in 1893. P. C. Edwards said that at ten past seven on Boxing Day, when in the company of P. S. Thomas, he saw Jones in King Street. He was staggering and behaving indecently. After a little persuasion he went home. He was fined ten shillings.

William Henry Watkins was also summoned for being drunk and disorderly at Blaenavon. He pleaded guilty. P. C. Love said that at quarter to ten on the night in question he saw Watkins in Avon Road near the residence of Mr White, the Gas Works. He was drunk and wanted someone to come out of the house to fight him. This was his first appearance and he was fined five shillings.

The Llangibby Hounds met at Llangibby Castle in 1901, where Dr. and Ms Rutherford Harris entertained about eighty members of the Llangibby, Monmouthshire and Tredegar hunts to breakfast in the house while in the grounds about a thousand footmen and friends of the hunt were entertained in marquees. Lord Tredegar was unfortunately not able to be present. After breakfast a move was made to Coed-y-paen where a fox was found, though the hounds did not follow. Another fox was hunted for over two hours in the forest when he broke cover and made for Llangibby Park. He then crossed the river and the hounds were called off.

In 1906 a rugby match was played between Monmouth and South Africa, in Newport. The Springboks won, 17 - 0

NEW YEAR

In 1805, the Cambrian newspaper published a lesson for the new year, resolutions were just as much a part of our ancestors lives as they are today.

"Begin the year with an impartial review of past life and with a sincere and firm resolution to rectify whatever has been amiss.

If you have hitherto been slumbering in indolence, it is now time to wake out of sleep; for much is to be done and the time to do it in is short. If the poisonous weeds of vice have been sprouting up in your mind, resolve now to eradicate them. If you have been addicted to profane swearing, to using the cup of intemperance, or to any other practice that degrades the human character, and wastes your estate, improve the present opportunity to beak the pernicious spell and to deliver yourself from the pit of ruin.

If you have neglected to govern and educate your children in such a manner as tends to lead them in the practice of good morals, turn over a new leaf and for the future let your example and precepts combine in training them up in the way they should go.

Regulate your expenses according to your income. If that be small, carefully study economy and let industry supply the deficiency. If you are one of the ton, or a leader of fashion, try, for once to make good morals fashionable. If you have been raised to any considerable office consider that your example will tend either to purify or to poison the manners of others and that if you set an ill example you will be answerable even for its remotest consequences. If you are rich, open your hearts to deeds of charity and benevolence. Extend a liberal hand to the children of need, that the blessing of such as are ready to perish may come upon you. Devote some of the surplusage of your income to the education of the children of the poor, who may thankfully rise up and call you blessed. In a word, study to be good and do good. Let every day be marked with deeds of virtue and then on the last day of this year, peaceful reflections will soothe your mind; or even if death should intervene before the sun should perform another annual revolution, the testimony of a good conscience will be better than the softest down to your pillow and will support you in the last struggles of nature".

The Mari Llwyd was a feature of New Year in Wales and it was reported in 1838 that it -

"continues to delight young and old every winter in Pontypool, Govilon and Abergavenny. The parties go about, singing Welsh songs and dance, the horse well skilled in frightening maidens who peep through half open doors. St George and the dragon is still to be seen on the hills but not so numerous as horses".

New Year was a time for entertainment and in 1849 the first meeting of the Cwmbran Cymraegyddion Society took place at the Halfway House. There was a 'goodly muster of the fair sex' and a large gathering of bards from various parts of Wales. Harpist, David Davies of

Gellygaer was present. The meeting was at four in the afternoon but groups had arrived before then until about three hundred people were present. Mr Blewitt won first prize for the best ode.

Mr Thomas Bowen, a contractor from Blaenavon, provided his men, numbering about sixty five to a supper of roast beef and plum pudding in 1850. He also provided each man with one quart of Christmas beer and about ten o clock they parted wishing Mr Bowen prosperity and long life and gratitude for his kindness.

New Years Eve 1857 was unseasonably mild. On the last day and following morning the sun rose as if it was a spring day and not a cloud was seen in the sky. On New Years Eve there were many suppers, balls and card parties. Among the most prominent, as there were too many to mention, was the quadrille ball and card party at the Kings Head Inn, Cross Street. The party of thirty couples met and began 'amusements'. An excellent band was in attendance and for several hours festivities continued. An interval saw all the delicacies of the season served. While eating, many toasts were given then dancing resumed until an early hour the following day.

A numerous party assembled at Mr Anthony's Horseshoe Inn, Pontnewynydd in 1858. There were excellent musicians in attendance and dancing commenced and continued until a late hour. The wines were of a superior quality and a very agreeable evening was spent.

1859 was ushered in quietly in Pontypool according to the Monmouthshire Merlin. The first sign of its presence was observed in a group of youths scrambling for a few pence which some shopkeepers had distributed amongst them. It was a custom that young people received gifts of money, fruit, nuts, oranges or cake from local tradesmen. Later in the morning a drum and fife band arrived from Abercarn and paraded the streets at intervals until the return train at three o clock.. A canvas covered theatre was being built where 'Lord Lovel and the Mistletoe Bough' was being performed. Here and there people wished each other 'the compliments of the season' and New Year gifts were exchanged though these were becoming smaller and much less. In the evening several parties were held. The choir of the High Street Wesleyan Chapel sang several selections from The Messiah, at Pontypool Park, the echo of which reverberated in the streets. During the week housewives removed holly and evergreens from their homes and hung their new Merlin sheet Almanacs over the old ones,.

The custom of watching in the new year was observed in the Town School, Pontypool in 1861 when an address was delivered by the Reverend Dovey.

1864 was welcomed in Blaenavon by merry peals from the church bells which were kept ringing at intervals until two o clock in the morning. Watch Night services had been held at the Wesleyan Primitive Methodist Chapels and appropriate addresses at places of worship.

In 1865, as a consequence of New Years Eve being on a Sunday it was not celebrated with the usual festivity. Watch Night meetings were held in various churches and the choirs sang anthems at the doors of friends reminding them of the approach of 1866. The new year brought boisterous weather on the hills, rain, snow and hail followed in quick succession

On New Years Day 1868 a large number of spectators assembled in a field near the Rock and Fountain public house to witness a coursing match. There was a good crowd who enjoyed the sport.

Watch Night was explained in a little more detail in the Monmouthshire Merlin in 1870. It was a custom of the Wesleyan Methodists to hold the Watch Night service. A feature was to spend the last few minutes of the old year in silent prayer. As the hour of midnight approached, until a minute or two before twelve, all was hushed into silence. When the meeting point of the two years passed all rose and sang the hymn 'Come let us anew our journey pursue'.

This service was held at Wesley Chapel Newport and Victoria Chapel Maindee where sermons were preached and addresses delivered.

The old year of 1870 went out amid musical celebrations in Ebbw Vale. Bands and choirs paraded the streets until 1870 had run its course. There were also the usual midnight services.

For new year 1875 a treat was given to the inmates of Monmouth Union workhouse. A well stocked Christmas tree was provided for the children and more substantial amusements for the adults. One of the inmates, aged 102, usually favoured visitors with a dance but was too ill to do so this year. Mr Hodson exhibited a magic lantern. Reverend Warlow gave a lecture then music and dancing was kept up until a late hour.

In Pontnewydd, in 1879, a tea meeting was held and in the evening a New Year tree with a great variety of useful articles exhibited. It was a great success and the response from the public was 'gratifying'.

New Year was celebrated in Ebbw Vale in 1881 with midnight services held in all the Wesleyan and Primitive Methodist chapels. The 'Salvation Army' corps held what they designated 'a night with Jesus'. The Monmouthshire Merlin recorded that strange scenes were reenacted, but didn't specify what, and that the meeting didn't break up until dawn.

New Year in Pontypool in 1887 was ushered in in a quiet manner and with less ceremony than in years gone by. The evening was bitterly cold with a keen frost and the area was enveloped in fog. The town however was busy until a late hour and while young people went carolling from door to door, bands of musicians wandered the town making it a lively place until well after the new year arrived. As no bells rang to signal the new year, the sounds of hooters from distant collieries took over the task. Watch services took place but, they were becoming popular among all sorts of religious people as well as Wesleyans and despite the freezing cold many places of worship were full. At the Primitive Methodist chapel, Park Terrace, a coffee supper was held followed by a service. The Hanbury Volunteer Band had a dinner and social gathering and the Pontypool Glee Party held a similar event. New Year's Day was dry and fine, bands of musicians played through the district. An old saying, according to the Pontypool Free Press was that if New Year's Day fell on a Saturday, as it did in 1887, there would be a mild winter, a hot summer and a late harvest.

In 1908 an article by 'Cadrawd' was published in the Cardiff Times concerning old Welsh customs and wassailing in Gwent. Canu Cwnsela was a New Year greeting performed by the old inhabitants of the county. In the time when the custom was carried out properly, there was much preparation. First the head of a horse was decorated with ribbons of many colours after the skull had been draped in white calico. The bottoms of two glass bottles were fitted in the eye sockets and ears were cut from black shoe leather. Beneath the drapery was the bearer of the Mari Llwyd whose duty was to animate the horse and perform bows outside the door of those visited and after entering it was made to dance to the tune of a harp. A ring formed in the middle of the room and after the performance a cap was put in the mare's mouth for donations with a bow for each one. Children were afraid of the Mari and Cadrawd recalled being terrified as a boy.

Before entering the house the door was bolted and the group would exchange verses with the occupants inside. Each party answered in rhyme. This exchange could last over an hour. An answer had to be made within a minute and produced in Wales a class of men known as 'men of the ready muse'. Before leaving the house, after the group had entertained, the wassailing bowl with its eighteen handles was brought to the table and filled with mead or beer and served with Christmas cake. Blessings were also sang to the family of the house.

TWELFTH NIGHT

Twelfth Night is so called, according to Horatio Smith who wrote to the Monmouthshire Merlin in 1839, because it is the twelfth day after the Nativity when the eastern magi were guided by the star to the baby Jesus. The festive customs of Twelfth Night were originally intended to represent the magi who were supposed to be kings. In France one of the courtiers was formally chosen to be king and waited upon by the monarch in a role reversal situation. In Germany a similar custom existed among the scholars of colleges and civic banquets. At our own colleges and in private entertainments Smith says it was customary to give the name of the king to the person whose portion of divided cake, (the Twelfth Night cake), contained a lucky bean or royal inscribed label and honour him in a mock homage. The remembrance of the eastern kings seems to have been borrowed from the Roman Saturnalia when the masters made a banquet for their servants and waited upon them; and partly from the Roman custom of drawing lots or beans for the title of king, when the fortunate party was declared king of the festivities and exercised full authority until they separated. Besides a bean, a pea was sometimes put in for a queen.

Mentions of Twelfth Night celebrations in Monmouthshire's old newspapers tend to concentrate on the festivities of Tredegar House. One of the earliest is from the Cambrian newspaper in 1819. Here it is called Old Christmas Day (before the calendar Act in 1751 Christmas was celebrated on the equivalent of the 6th January by our modern calendar). It was marked with extensive hospitality by Sir Charles Morgan. Races took place between amateur jockeys in the park which was attended by a very large crowd. The cup was won by Mr George Morgan riding his own chestnut horse.

By 1831 the festivities were being described in slightly more detail. It was the custom of Sir Charles's family and friends, stated the Monmouthshire Merlin to partake of his hospitality on Twelfth Day. At one in the afternoon the races began. There were four horses who started for the Sir Charles cup which was won by Mr Morgan. The Ladies cup was won by Mr Mitchell's horse, Hussar. At dinner, a numerous party from the neighbourhood joined and a ball and supper was held until a late hour. Sir Charles was not unmindful of the poor and a large party returned from the house with warm clothing distributed among them by Sir Charles.

Sir Charles Morgan wasn't the only one looking out for the poor on Old Christmas Day. Thomas Powell of the Gaer House, Newport, distributed to the poor of Newport and St Woollos in 1836 one ton and four hundred weight of bread to a great many families. Mr Powell had been elected to the council and chosen to be alderman of the borough.

Unfortunately later accounts of the gatherings at Tredegar House, give no mention of donating to the poor, though that doesn't mean it wasn't happening, it just wasn't reported. One hundred ladies and gentlemen were present at the house in 1856. The Monmouthshire Merlin described it as an interesting event, the writer gushing at the richness and elegance of the costumes, the attractiveness of fancy dress and military uniform. The band of the Clare militia performed in the orchestra, it was their first time performing at a festive event. At the announcing of supper, the banqueting room was opened which presented a scene of great splendour. Among the many varieties of food stood the Twelfth Night cake, displaying the flags of the allied nations, while down the sides of tables were names of principle eastern victories. The relevance of the flags being the involvement of Sir Charles's son Godfrey in the Crimean War. After supper, dancing continued for many hours.

Celebrations in 1862 were kept to a minimum, in respect of the memory of the Prince Consort and in sympathy with Queen Victoria. The number of visitors was comparatively limited and though races took place in the park, no public festivities were held. A party assembled at the house but it was strictly private and mostly of a family nature.

1863 was back to normal with Lord Tredegar gathering a group of friends ranking in the same station as himself, for festivities. Races were held and despite the rain and drizzle, visitors trudged along the road, ankle deep in mud. Those who could took their carriages. The Merlin reported the usual amount of 'strange looking edibles and fruit'. Traders were present in the grounds and everywhere was the deafening cries of 'Oranges! Fine oranges!' and 'Pies! All hot!'.

Owing to the rain the ground was heavy and only the strongest horse stood any chance of winning. There were one hundred and forty guests for the Ball. It took place in a spacious ballroom with massive mirrors, brilliant illuminations and artistically designed decorations to resemble fairyland. Costumes were worn, ranging from Marie Antoinette to a Welsh fisherwoman.

Members of the principle families in both

Monmouthshire and Glamorgan responded to the invitation of Lady Tredegar to attend festivities in 1869. As well as the usual races those who attended the Ball dressed as characters from the pages of history and fiction and the powdering of hair was much resorted to. Some of the costumed guests were Lord Tredegar, Hereford Hunt Club; Lady Tredegar, a lady of the time of George II; Mrs F C Morgan, Cinderella's godmother; Mr Hanbury Leigh, a Knight Templar; Miss Crawshay, Queen of Peacocks; Mr A Brewer, Russian peasant and Miss Brewer, also a peasant.

The following year, the Merlin reported that the races, did not take place on the day of the Ball but were announced for the following day.

By 1871 it is only the Twelfth Night Ball that is being recorded in the local newspapers. They describe draped and lighted rooms with guests arriving at around ten o clock at night in fancy dress. There was an interval for supper. The supper room was tastefully laid out with Lord Tredegar's prize plate and display of silver exhibited in one part of the room.

Guests were even more numerous and costumes more elegant in 1873. A 'princely' reception for the guests was held in the ballroom. Gentlemen and Ladies were received by Lord and Lady Tredegar. There were costumes in every variety and colour and music, dancing and supper on a table laid out in an attractive manner with elaborate decorations. A Twelfth Night cake on which the greatest care and skill had been bestowed was the centrepiece. Music was performed by Messrs Pollock and Jacobs String band. As well as the Ball for the rich, the servants had their own Ball at which around two hundred attended.

WAR

The origin of the First World War can be attributed to a trigger event that happened on 28 June 1914, the assassination of Archduke Franz Ferdinand who had been on his way to inspect troops in Bosnia. On 4th August 1914, Britain declared war on Germany and by December about a million volunteers had signed up to fight, expecting the war to be over by Christmas, except, it wasn't.

The 2nd Monmouthshire Regiment was in France on 6th November 1914 at Le Havre. War diaries mention deficiencies in equipment and boots. This led to people back home raising funds to provide the soldiers of all three Monmouthshire regiments with essential items that they lacked, as seen in a letter to Mrs Martin of Abergavenny on 18th December 1914.

"Dear Mrs Martin – The large bale of shirts, socks and mufflers arrived safely, for which, please accept our very grateful thanks. It is simply wonderful how cheerful the men are under such trying circumstances and it is very kind of you all to think of them. We are trying to give them a sort of 'bean feast' on Christmas Day thanks to the generous spirit of the good people of Abergavenny and round the farms here. Yours Truly, Lieutenant A Fry, 3rd Monmouthshire Regiment."

From December 14th to the 29th, the 2nd Monmouthshire Regiment occupied the same line of trenches as the Essex Regiment, rotating every four days, near Frelinghien. The 2nd Monmouthshire's were relieved by the Essex Regiment on Christmas Day evening but before that, something wonderful and unique happened that has never been repeated.

Christmas morning, 1914 began with the Germans singing Silent Night. A local armistice had been agreed upon, no one would fire that day. The men from the 2nd Monmouthshire's sang Hark the Herald Angels, back. This appeared to surprise the Germans, so one of the soldiers and a sergeant, William Jones, got hold of a copy of the Free Press, dated 11th December and attached it to the top of a rifle as a flag of truce. All firing had stopped so the men peered out to have a look and found the Germans sat on top of their trenches, about fifty yards away, waving and asking if they had any cigarettes. So William and the other soldier gathered some up, as well as some tins of jam, climbed out of their trench and walked towards them. The German officers wouldn't let their men leave their trench so the cigarettes and food was thrown over.

The Germans were the 7th Bavarian regiment with whom the men spent a peaceful couple of hours. This gave them the chance to bury the dead and there are accounts of each side working together to achieve this, even holding services.

Of course the truce didn't last. William mentions a friend of his in one of his letters home who did the same as he did, a bit further down the line. After the Germans had taken the tobacco and he was on his return to his trench, they shot him in the back and killed him.

Signaller, Edwin Pearce of W company, 2nd Monmouthshire's describes his experiences of Christmas 1914 in a letter to his parents at 5 Richmond Road, Abergavenny.

"I enjoyed my Christmas day all right. I was lucky to be at head quarters and not with the battalion as they were in the trenches on that day and lost a few more men. One sergeant got shot on Christmas Day. While I and my mates were at head quarters learning the telegraph work, we were attached to the Royal Engineers and was with them over Christmas. We had a fine time. There were about a hundred of us sat down to dinner. We had geese, three pieces of roast beef and potatoes, so we had a good feed all in style, with a table too and plenty of pudding. We had tea in style too and a smoking concert from 6.30 until 11 pm; plenty of fags and tobacco and food and a good sing song. There were about two hundred at the concert, they had three barrels of beer between them and I believe I was the only teetotaller there – a bit dry, but grand I can assure you. I am in the pink and feel fit for anything that comes along. I expect I shall have to join the battalion next time they go in the trenches but I am not sure."

Mr Morris of the Temperance Hotel, Abergavenny received a letter from Corporal Bert Watkins of the 2nd Monmouthshire's. Watkins was a resident of Pontypool and was at Armentieres.

"I had rather a novel experience on Christmas day. We received orders from the Brigadier not to fire unless we were bound to, so we got quite pally with the Germans, shaking hands and a lot of other things. One chap gave a tin of No. 1 army rations. You should have seen him collect it and put it in his pocket as if he was starving. I will bet he enjoyed his Christmas dinner in the trenches, different to what we did. Rather a funny day for burying the dead isn't it? But they had a few too, I promise you. On our left there were dozens of them stretched out; in fact so many they could not bury all yesterday (Christmas day). There is only about fifty yards between us, you should hear the compliments passing. That crack regiment the Prussian Guards were there when we went in and when we shouted out they called us '.....fools'. You don't believe we are that, do you? They were changed about the 23rd by a lot of old men and boys by what I could see of them. I expect they think we will take pity on them, but that is just the sort I like to fight, don't you?"

Corporal Yearsley of Abercarn described similar events in a letter to his wife at 40 Canal Row.

"We had the time of our lives on Christmas Day. The Germans got out of their trenches without their rifles and walked half way across the field to where our trenches were. There was not a shot fired. Some of our chaps got out and went and met them and you ought to have seen the result. They started shaking hands and giving smokes to our chaps. There was a nice bit of singing on both sides. They walked and talked with one another as if there were nothing the matter. Our chaps helped them to bury the dead and sang over them afterwards. It was a thing which those who saw it will never forget".

Mary Steel was the driving force behind fund raising efforts in Abergavenny and in January 1915 she thanked all those, via local newspaper, who had supported her appeal.

"I should like to thank all those who kindly responded to my appeal to send Christmas puddings to the men of the 3rd Monmouthshire's at Grundisburgh near Suffolk. I enclose a letter from Colonel Worsley Gough who commands the battalion.

'Will you accept yourself and convey to all those who have so kindly contributed towards the men's Christmas cheer, their grateful thanks for all that has been done. The men have for some time been doing very hard and uninspiring work under the worst possible weather conditions and the kind thoughts for their welfare at Christmas time cheered them immensely. The balance of the money which has kindly been remitted shall be expended for the benefit of the men'.

Christmas 1915, it wasn't just the soldiers in the

trenches who funds were being raised for, but also prisoners of war. The Abergavenny and District Licensed Victuallers Association at their monthly meeting in October 1915 discussed a novel way to help the fund for Monmouthshire prisoners of war and to ensure they had some Christmas cheer to remind them of the festive season. It was suggested that members should subscribe to the purchase of a bullock which would be decorated and sold at the Christmas market under the hammer of Straker, Son and Chadwick. The proceeds from this sale would then go to the fund. Subscribers were entitled to name the recipients of parcels among the prisoners of war according to the amount of their subscription. The Association adopted the suggestion and Mr Chadwick made the necessary arrangements.

In November 1915, Mary Steele, with Marion Whitehead, once again made an appeal through local newspapers for help to send the 3rd Monmouthshire's, who were now in France, Christmas puddings. She said

"We want to make their Christmas as bright as possible and let them know we have not forgotten them and all they are doing for us".

The girls of the Victoria Street Council School gave an entertainment in the school room in December 1915, in aid of the Monmouthshire Prisoner of War Fund. It was called a volunteer entertainment from the fact the girls carried it out by themselves. They sang 'I'd like to be a Soldier' and the Empire Song. Recitations were give by Ena Brown, Irene Viney, Flo James, Kathleen Watkins, Muriel Morris, Annie Norman and Miss H Gardner. Pianoforte performances were given by Doris Wibberley, Marjorie Price and May Cowley. Seven girls performed an amusing sketch called 'A Christmas Wait'.

Major Williams gave an address and Mr W Jacobs said he was pleased to find they were doing their bit to help prisoners of war and he was sure they would enjoy Christmas all the better for it. Miss Baldwin said the teachers had done nothing to help the children except for some pupil teachers who had helped in the sketch.

In February 1916, the Committee of the Monmouthshire regimental agency of the Prisoner of War help Committee reported that the number of prisoners of war for the 1st and 3rd battalions on their books was 284 and regular fortnightly parcels were being sent out. For Christmas the committee was able to send a special parcel of plum pudding with a Christmas card with greeting, vests, pants, woollen gloves, biscuits, tins of beef, sardines, oxo cubes, cocoa, condensed milk, sugar, tea, golden syrup, potted meat, carbolic soap and fifty cigarettes, the money for which was collected by Miss Llewellin and Miss Sasha Murphy. Besides food, each man was sent a complete outfit of clothing, great coat, coat and trousers, cardigan, shirts, vests and shoes. Boots were being sent later.

The men replied to say how thankful they were for all that was being done. They were delighted with their Christmas puddings and the warm clothing as the weather had been bitterly cold and many said they were almost in rags. Where men had not been traced or had died, the parcels were returned from Germany, unopened and in good condition.

Another appeal was made by Mary Steel in October 1916 to local newspapers. It read

"Dear Sir, I have been asked by the Prisoners Aid Committee to collect money to enable every man of the 3rd Monmouthshire Regiment who is a prisoner in Germany to have a plum pudding at Christmas. The puddings will be made in Newport and sent direct to each man. This was done last year and the men felt they were not forgotten".

By November 1917, funds were running low and another appeal was made.

"More help is needed so that Monmouthshire Prisoners of War shall not be deprived of parcels they look forward to. Monmouthshire Prisoners of War Regimental Care Committee have done excellent work keeping the men from starvation and protecting them from weather by sending them food and clothing. It costs over £100 a week to send parcels and there are only three weeks funds left. The committee desire to send special parcels for Christmas and £1000 is needed. There is no need to expatiate on the terrible conditions of prisoners in the hands of the enemy."

In Llantilio Pertholey a house to house collection for the purpose of raising funds to provide Christmas parcels for the men from the parish serving at home or abroad was well supported. There were one hundred men serving their country while eighty of those were abroad. The collection totalled £38 and enabled a good parcel to be sent to each man. It was decided to send to each man a parcel to the value of eight shillings if abroad and four shillings if home. The subscription remained open for a few days afterwards for any further donations that could cover the cost of postage.

1918, war was over but it didn't mean the instant return of men back to Monmouthshire. A notice was printed in the South Wales Daily Post that preference in Christmas leave would be given to youths of eighteen and men of 40 who were married. Extra leave was given to men who had joined up in 1914. Many faced another Christmas overseas and the Monmouth Guardian printed dates by which parcels had to be posted.

"Christmas parcels for our soldiers – The Postmaster General calls attention to the necessity of posting all letters and parcels intended for delivery to the troops in France, Belgium, Germany and Italy by Christmas Day, not later than the following dates – Italian force: parcels December 9th; letters December 16th. British force: parcels December 14th; letters December 16th."

Relief at the end of war prevailed throughout the county and land and can be seen in simple phrases such as this one from the Monmouth Guardian on 20 December 1918.

"After the dark Decembers of the last four seasons it is a pleasure merely to walk through the lighted streets once more, and to gaze on the brilliant display in the shop windows worthily arranged for a Peace Christmas"

MISCELLANEOUS

Not quite Christmas, but in late January 1869 Charles Dickens visited Newport and read 'A Christmas Carol' and the Trial from Pickwick at the Victoria Rooms. There was a crowded house and Charles Dickens received quite an ovation from his appearance stated the Pontypool Free Press.

Not in Monmouthshire but this ancient custom was printed in the Monmouthshire Merlin in 1878.

On the eve of Old Christmas Day there are thirteen fires lighted in the cornfields of many of the farms, twelve of them in a circle and one round a pole, much longer and higher than the rest, in the centre. These fires are dignified with the names of the Virgin Mary and twelve apostles, the lady being in the middle. While they are burning the labourers retire into some shed or out house where they can watch the brightness of the flames. Into this shed they lead a cow, on whose horn a large plum cake has been stuck and, having assembled round the animal, the oldest labourer takes a pail of cider and addresses the following lines to the cow with great solemnity, after which the same verse is chanted in chorus by all present:-

'Here's to thy pretty face and milk white horn,
Heaven send thy master a good crop of corn
Both wheat, rye and barley – all sorts of grain ·
And next year, if we live, we'll drink to thee again.'

He then dashes the cider in the cows face, when, by a violent toss of her head, she throws the plumcake on the ground and if it falls forward it is an omen that the next harvest will be good; if backward that it will be unfavourable. This is the ceremony at the commencement of the rural feast which is generally prolonged until the following morning.

In December 1919 an Italian professor prophesied that the end of the world would occur on the 17th December. No one knew how he got his information but the ladies of Abergavenny were so alarmed that they postponed the making of their Christmas puddings until the 18th while others, who had made theirs, thought it was best to eat them beforehand!

REFERENCES

Monmouthshire Merlin
Pontypool Free Press
South Wales Daily News
Tell Them of Us – Carol Ann Lewis
Evening Express
The Cambrian
The Weekly Mail
Victorian Cwmbran – Carol Ann Lewis
Victorian Pontypool – Carol Ann Lewis
Monmouth Gazette
Cardiff Times

ABOUT THE AUTHOR

Carol Ann Lewis was born in South Wales in 1969. She is the current secretary of Cwmbran Writers Group and has contributed to their publications as well as writing her own books. She has also written local history for a Cwmbran newsletter. She enjoys writing fiction, ghost stories and history and often dabbles with all three at the same time! She has four children and six grandchildren.

'Like' me on Facebook

or

Follow me on Twitter @carolannlewis1

www.ingramcontent.com/pod-product-compliance
Lightning Source LLC
Chambersburg PA
CBHW072014290526
45787CB00013B/911